The bilby is a nocturnal Australian mammal.

Before the arrival of European settlers, two types of bilbies lived on mainland Australia: the greater bilby and the lesser (or little) bilby. The lesser bilby is probably extinct. It was last seen in 1931. The greater bilby is also vulnerable to extinction due to habitat reduction. It lives secretly in several remote arid and semi-arid areas, including a region in the north of Western Australia called the Pilbara — the setting of this story.

You are unlikely to see the greater bilby in the wild, but at Easter, in Australia, you can see chocolate bilbies everywhere, rapidly replacing chocolate Easter bunnies.

For Kaitlin, Kirralee, and Kalina — E. W.

*For Bob and Jan Standaloft and all those who
dedicate their time to save our wildlife — M. J.*

First U.S. edition 2015

Library of Congress Catalog Card Number 2013955950
ISBN 978-0-7636-6759-7

SCP 19 18 17 16 15 14
10 9 8 7 6 5 4 3 2 1

Printed in Humen, Dongguan, China

This book was typeset in Tempus Sans ITC and Fairfield LH.
The illustrations were done in mixed media.

Candlewick Press
99 Dover Street
Somerville, Massachusetts 02144

visit us at www.candlewick.com

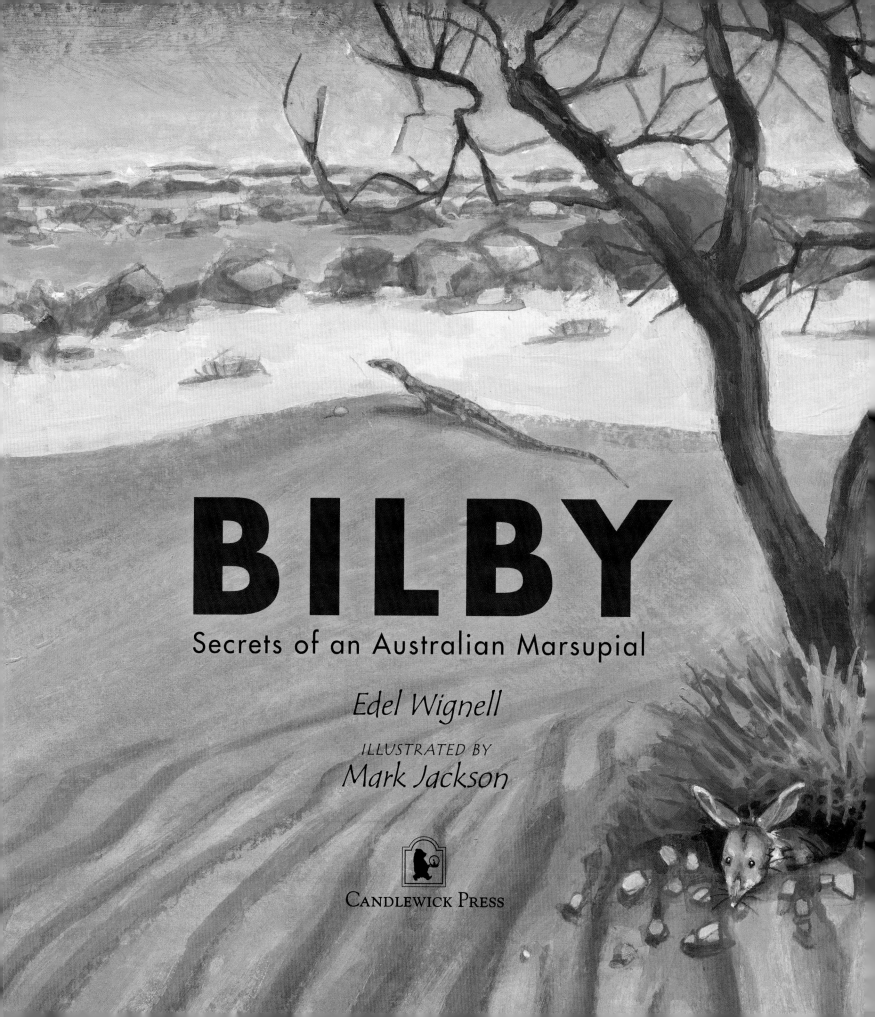

BILBY

Secrets of an Australian Marsupial

Edel Wignell

ILLUSTRATED BY
Mark Jackson

CANDLEWICK PRESS

In the moonlight, Bilby canters—
tail aloft like a banner—across the spiny grass and
enters a steeply sloping, spiral tunnel. She flings the dirt back,
her hind feet together, closing the entrance to her burrow.

It's time for the birth of her baby.

Bilbies dig their burrows in clay or loam or stone instead of
sand. The burrows are about six and a half feet (two meters)
underground and are about ten feet (three meters) long.

1

Bilby squats on her hind legs and tail, with her head on her front paws. She folds her ears forward, creating a cocoon of silence. When Baby Bilby is born, he is as long as your little toe. He crawls up his mother's fur and into her warm, dark pouch. He grasps a nipple and sucks.

Bilbies have litters of one, two, or, occasionally, three babies. The young are safe in the pouch, which opens backward so that it doesn't fill with dirt when the mother digs.

When Bilby wakes, she's hungry. She waits until
darkness descends to leave the burrow, pausing
for a moment at the tunnel entrance.

She listens! She sniffs! In her pouch,
Baby sleeps on, unaware.

Bilbies have poor eyesight, but their senses of hearing and
smell are acute, so they constantly listen and sniff for danger.

5

Bilby canters across the sand.

She noses between rocks where eight-legged morsels hide.
Succulent spiders!

Bilby stops and checks for danger. Hearing an owl, she hisses,
then dashes into the nearest tunnel, kicking the dirt back.

The frantic movements wake Baby, but he is safe in the
pouch. He suckles and sleeps, suckles and sleeps.

If a predator, such as an owl, eagle, fox, dingo, or feral cat, catches a bilby, the bilby will fight. It bites with its sharp teeth, kicks with its strong back legs, and tears with the claws of its front paws.

Baby Bilby grows and grows. At last, it's time for adventure. He crawls out of the pouch.

First he sniffs and explores his mother: her long, silky fur; naked, rabbit-like ears; long muzzle; and crested tail with its horny spur at the tip.

Then he discovers his underground home. He searches it from top to bottom.

After about seventy-five days, a bilby is ready to leave its mother's pouch. A mother may have four litters each year.

For two weeks, Bilby leaves her baby in the burrow while she forages for food. She returns from time to time to suckle him.

Young Bilby explores and sleeps, explores and sleeps. He grows. He exercises in his playground—the burrow. He dashes around and scuttles across. He stretches high. Soon he will be ready for the world of bilby adults.

Bilbies eat termites, insects and their larvae, spiders, fungi, tubers, and seeds — depending on the season. Most of the moisture they need comes from their food.

Finally the time has come for
Young Bilby to leave his cool
burrow. His mother pauses at
the entrance. She listens and
sniffs—alert. Young Bilby
listens and sniffs, too.

Suddenly, he is aware of the warm night air,
of space and sky, of moon and starlight.
Bilby canters, and he follows. They forage
in the underground passages of a mound
and crunch a tasty termite feast.

12

Bilbies have sharp teeth.
As they hunt, they store
food in their cheeks.

All night Young Bilby moves about, foraging. His mother is constantly alert, and Young Bilby mimics her. He learns that she has many tunnels. He learns that when she senses danger, they must dash into the nearest one.

14

A bilby may have up to twenty tunnels in its feeding area, and never feeds more than about three hundred feet (one hundred meters) from a tunnel.

The night is filled with shadows.

Young Bilby leaves his mother and forages alone.
Free at last! He pauses frequently, listens and sniffs.
He sees the shining eyes of other bilbies and the eight
eyes of a golden orb-weaver, reflecting the moonlight.

Digging for food,
bilbies leave pits up to four inches
(ten centimeters) deep in the soil.

He sees two still, glowing points in the rocks—
the eyes of a fox. Young Bilby dives into the nearest tunnel.
He kicks frantically. He waits—breathing fast, heart thudding.

Later, he emerges and feeds until dawn, then returns
to the hiding burrow. For the first time, he sleeps alone.

The steep, spiral descent of bilbies' tunnels makes it difficult for predators to follow them.

19

The next night, Young Bilby canters farther and farther away from his mother. She ignores him. He digs for tubers, and feasts.

He hears a soft *Shh! Shh!* With undulating movements, an olive python comes closer and closer. *Shh! Shh!*

Startled, Young Bilby hisses. He digs with the sharp claws of his strong front paws. He kicks the dirt back with his powerful hind legs. He scrabbles furiously, entering the earth like a corkscrew. Safe! Then he begins to dig a burrow—his first, his own.

Bilbies are efficient burrowers, able to disappear from sight in three minutes.

21

Young Bilby squats on his haunches and takes a deep breath.
Now fully grown, he has learned the secrets of surviving
in his desert home.

When a bilby male is six to seven months old, he finds a female and they
mate in a burrow. Three weeks later he becomes a father, but he doesn't
take care of his baby. He will be solitary all his life, except when he mates.

INDEX

babies 1, 3, 5, 6, 9, 22

burrows 1, 5, 10, 12, 18, 21, 22

claws 7, 21

digging 1, 3, 17, 20–21

ears 3, 9

food 9, 10–11, 13, 17

legs 3, 7, 21

pouch 3, 6, 9

predators 7, 19

senses 5, 14

sleeping 5, 6, 10, 18

tails 1, 3, 9

teeth 7, 13

tunnels 1, 5, 6, 14–15, 18–19

Look up the pages to find out about all these bilby things.

Don't forget to look at both kinds of words—

this kind and this kind.